David Bowerbank was raised in Scarborough; however, he spent many years on the streets inclusive of time at her then Majesty's pleasure for vagrancy incorporating nuisance value. From an early age, he displayed an outstanding talent for literature, especially poetry. His work provides an eye-opening insight into the depths of deprivation vagrancy can produce plus the inevitable Northern humour.

To my wife, Sue, without you, I wouldn't be here.

David Bowerbank

I Saw a Little Fox

AUSTIN MACAULEY PUBLISHERS™
LONDON * CAMBRIDGE * NEW YORK * SHARJAH

A CIP catalogue record for this title is available from the British Library.

ISBN 9781035851614 (Paperback)
ISBN 9781035851621 (Hardback)
ISBN 9781035851645 (ePub e-book)
ISBN 9781035851638 (Audiobook)

www.austinmacauley.com

First Published 2024
Austin Macauley Publishers Ltd®
1 Canada Square
Canary Wharf
London
E14 5AA

Mr Grant, my English teacher

Johnny Young, my earliest friend

Scarborough Athletic F.C.

I saw a little fox today as clear as plain could be
He pulled up on his bicycle and said hello to me.
His fur was bright and shiny, his teeth were pearly white,
A little out of character as the vulpine prowls at night,
I petted his fat belly and stroked his tiny head,
Then carried him into the woods and put him back to bed.

When you are homeless you lose all your pride,
When you are homeless you don't live inside,
When you are homeless you don't kiss the bride,
Nobody to turn to, nowhere to hide,
When you are homeless you sleep in a box,
Can't pay for a haircut, can't afford socks,
When you are homeless your sleeve is a tissue,
When you are homeless you sell the Big Issue,
When you are homeless it messes up your head,
When you are homeless you don't own a bed,
When you are homeless your self-esteem tumbles,
Your skin starts to scab your oesophagus rumbles,
When you are homeless you don't watch the telly,
As hunger pains pierce your back and your belly,
When you are homeless you gain notoriety,
A meaningless drain on a heartless society,
When you are homeless the affluent drones,
A bin-picking hobo for whom the bell tolls,
When you are homeless your naughty bits stink,
Please attempt to be homeless let me know what you think.

On coming back to Scarborough, Garfunkel oh so fair,
First thing that I noticed was a pub that wasn't there,
A broken heart was pending as I trundled on my way,
The football ground had crumbled where I saw a Charlton play,
Seamer Road no more my Manor, where Mam laid Billy Renton out with Dad's adjustable spanner,
No sweets shop no chippy no mutton dressed as lippy,
Where high hopes were nurtured for this alcoholic hippy,
My stomping ground; it was no more; no panes to smash no shithouse door,
No penny chews no bagatelle no scarpering when ringing the bell,
Time has come for me to flit
Desert this Yorkshire sinking ship On
quitting town I close the door Said
Hamlet ain't my home no more.

My Day By The Seaside,
Factor fifteen and a thingy,
Sixpence for machines some hand-down cut-off jeans and a shop-bought inflatable dinghy,
Mother bought a cornet whilst father had chips, just as Holding had Mike Brearley caught by Roberts in the slips,
Lunchtime came, oh what a treat, me mam had knocked up potted meat, with home-made parkin pigs in the gristle, the provvi man would have to whistle,
Just as we went crimson our mum granted a wish, lashings of ice cream in a Ravenhead dish, then father rolled his trousers up and poisoned all the fish,
Waves a lashing dodgems crashing sea fret lingers sugary fingers creepy crawlers bingo callers all the fun of the fair,
Time to hit the hay just as Coney Island closes, mother came through with donkey poo was a good year for the roses,
Mam's knotted hankey dad's string vest, my childhood really was the best.

Our queen she came to Scarborough,
I got the day off school,
Never seen somebody who was nearly born to rule,
We got there nice and early,
Me dad, he wore a tie,
Mother bought us Liquorice which we dipped inside a pie, With
bunting on the lampposts and hydrants painted green, Wasn't
it a dainty dish to set before a queen!
The cavalcade appeared and everybody cheered,
A black car gleaming clean, a monarch seldom seen, She went to
her reception with our mayor and thank you card, So I went back
and played with Jack in Johnny Young's back yard.

Being a hefty northerner there is one thing I can't do,
Can lay men out with just one clout and cook a rabbit stew,
Decimate three Shredded Wheat and belch a verse from Tiger Feet whilst
chewing sixteen Quality Street,
Ferret whippets cap on head, money safely under the bed,
There is a secret I must share, a local dish I can't prepare,
Every time I risk it, resembles a Rich Tea biscuit,
Now this may be a huge surprise, but my Yorkshire puddings will not rise, to an
acceptable sustainable regulatory size, So I'll stick to pies.

Whatever went wrong I will put it right,
Where there is day it will become night,
My mind broke free,
From being a homeless refugee,
What lies ahead because I know not where I'm going,
Totally misguided through my ambition overflowing,
As I co-exist with just a cardboard box surrounding me,
Clearly reflecting on a non-responsive family,
A head full to bursting with misleading information,
Showing my resentment for an ageing population,
Is time to accept that the fight is slowly faltering,
In retrospect, my journey is altering,
Allow them to rejoice and numb my voice,
Their life their rules; my destiny is their choice.

I once went to a football match; my team, they lost six four,
I didn't pay a penny as I sneaked in through the door,
Before half time, I bought a scarf and doughnuts from a van,
Just as my team appeared to Eton Rifles by the Jam,
Two penalties a sending off five bookings and a red,
Our burly centre forward wasted sitters with his head,
Defences ripped apart, fisticuffs at the memorabilia cart,
Away fans sensing blood because our approach play wasn't good, no midfield,
holes in the back lacking passion in attack,
The ref required glasses; our goalie broke a nail,
Their left winger, a real dead ringer for the Chairman at Port Vale,
Half time blown, the pies were hot,
First fan to refuse them was taken outside and shot,
Second stanza of this extravaganza,
Out to the strains of Mario Lanza,
Goal after goal destroyed soul after soul,
Paddy grazed the bar whilst Jock bereted VAR,
Pop goes the whistle we have lost to Partick Thistle,
Another defeat another reversal,
Relegation dress rehearsal,
The beautiful game, a working-class expression, And
the most common cause of severe depression.

Mum

You changed my dirty nappy,
You fed me in my cot,
You made my childhood happy,
Miss you quite a lot,
You tended to my grazes,
You often sang my praises,
You sacrificed your self-esteem,
You made sure all my clothes were clean,
You protected me you mothered me,
You respected me and smothered me,
I never came to any harm,
When wrapped around your maternal arm,
You set me free into a troubled society,
Through trepidation and sobriety,
You paid my rent you paid my fines,
You stopped me sniffing powdered lines, Till
the good lord whispered time to part, You broke my heart.

So this is Christmas
And what have you done
A celebration period for the good lord's only son
Arrives in mid-September, and hits you like a stone
Before you put the Branston out the Elves have sauntered home
Granny got her hold-ups, Grandad tripped on snuff
Toto got to Kansas 'coz the world is not enough
So I grabbed this opportunity from the bottom of my bike
To deliver season's greetings
Despite the postal strike

I thought I went to Wembley, to view a football game

Mansfield played a team from Spain with Betis in its name

Weather is quite Autumnal, with a long stud feel on top

Jack Cruxton bought a beanie from the souvenir shop

Early doors despite the roars the Stags were on the rack

Then Boycey broke a fracture in the centre forward's back

Tiny tiptoed down the wing as the underdogs began to sing

Minutes ticked down in London town as cheers rang out for Leicester, coz' the midfield bloke from downtown Stoke controlled that Iniesta

Extra time was looming as the Scotsman limbered up, Catalans were glooming as they sensed the game was up,

Scotty passed for Ginger who laid it back to Joss with Jonesy in the centre all it needed was a cross

Alfie was the target man who flicked the ball to Scott

Who left Iker Casillas rooted firmly to the spot

Upon the final whistle, Mansfield was victorious

We dare to dream about our team being happy and so glorious.

Our Mam, she kept a lovely house
We never smelt a stink
With Dairylea to the feed the mouse
And Stardrops round the sink
Carpet's never blemished
Drawers refused to dust
Windows never smeared and the gate refused to rust
Toilet hinted Lavender; the tiles they matched the floor
Rent man lost his sneakers
When collecting through the door
She didn't have no plug in's
Just Carbolic and a smile
Washing colours coordinate in a neatly folded pile
The local population
Knew Mam's battle with abrasion
So when stepping in the breach my old girl mopped it up, with Bleach.

He has no place in which to stay
So he lives in a doorway
The only pillow to place his head Is
a hard cold concrete bed

In all his clothing there is a tear
Thanks to long and constant wear
A long drawn face tells of struggle and strife Since
fate decided his way of life

From dirty hands, he eats his food
Is frowned upon as extremely rude
He has no part in life to play
Through our thoughtlessness, he has to pay.

Ladies and gentlemen next bout of the night
A fifteen-round contest world championship fight
The names are announced and a roar fills the air
As they enter the ring to a trumpet fanfare
Eagerly awaiting the fight to begin
Each hoping for the coveted crown he will win Hours
of training developing skill
Hoping one day they'll be topping the bill
Only a few eager fists make the grade
Contenders so far then eventually fade

Jason was our pussycat
She slept on a mat
I know she caught a mouse before
Not sure about a rat

When she was a kitten
She slept in Mother's boot
Right next to our coal fire
Yup, that ain't being no liar

Once she cut her mouth
In our backyard coal house
We bathed her face and put her right
The patient spent a comfortable night

She has had kittens the size of mittens
I think the kittens came from her
It's all rather wonderful
Praise the lord for creatures of fur

Lack of sleeps
My subconscious weeps
Brushed my teeth
Gargled with gin
Cooled the duvet
counted sheep
thought nice thoughts
wiggled my toes
changed my pyjamas
Powdered my nose
Iced the pillow
Swapped the sheet
Fed the cat
Ironed my feet
But sleep won't come
Into my head
So I dreamt I was awake
And went back to bed

Nor sat upon a jury available for hire
Can juggle crisps reverse a tank and chop stuff for the fire
Didn't go to college didn't qualify for glory
Never made my parents proud nor starred in Jackanory
Never asked to witness things nor view Nana Mouskouri
Never stood before three kings or sat on a jur
My life has been a travesty of steady starts and stutters
One petty thief two broken hearts and crashing out in gutters
When days are grim with no way out
Seek help be strong seek help and shout
The fog will clear the mist it shines Which
guided me to better times.

My mate Stan is quite the fella
Sups castor oil with vats of Stella
Can run a mile in next to nowt
Once turned a Python inside out
Head first off a concrete jetty
Flew solo to the Serengeti
Took Fury out with one big punch
Mad cow pie for Sunday lunch
Can kill a man with just his feet
Just the once consumed three Shredded Wheat
There is a secret we must keep
I am Stan whilst fast asleep
Wherever I go he goes, oh to be my alter ego

My daddy was a bigamist
With eight wives on the go
Two in Hull three in Istanbul
The others in Bromley by Bow
My poor Mum didn't have a clue
Coz we lived just north of Seaton Carew
Eleanor was number nine
In a short space of time
With number ten long overdue

On Friday we were moving
Oh yes, it is really true
Will be a funny feeling
Been there since seventy-two
Mother packed the sofa
My sister made the tea
Father a force in the Flying Horse
As he danced to Fiddler's three

Some stuff was discarded
Downsizing was a must
Mrs Hornby was red-carded
For mentioning the dust
Coffee tables TV cables
German helmets curtain pelmets
Plant pots Jelly Tots
Chair legs clothes pegs
Pack 'em in the crate
Removal men were late, so Mother packed the gate.

Since thumbing to the southern bit
Endured a lot of grief
From the way I shovel mulch to the gap between my teeth
Reside in caves and survive on tripe
Sending a pigeon our version of Skype
Unemployed towns hand me downs buckshee schools for dinners
An orderly queue for the outside loo whilst Grandad picked his winners
Boycott Hockney Sean Bean and slags
Compo Emmerdale and wacky baccy fags
I shall say this only once
Shall say it very loud
I come from Yorkshire
Stupid and proud

Not a Super Poet
Like to make words rhyme
Precisely why I have a bash at this from time to time
Will never be the Laureate
Strictly evictee
Discuss the toss with Mr Woss
Or appear on GMB
Far from humble to cavort in the jungle
Stick to the day job
Mustn't grumble
Conceived in somewhere by the sea
Complete my shift and home for tea

We owned a cat called Jason
Who lived till twenty-two!
She had a lot of kittens
Two rabbits and a shrew
Tortoiseshell golden locks
Our next-door neighbour poisoned her
So we put her in a box

Resided in some quirky towns
Explored this once-great nation
Hemel Hempstead Wooky Hole
Plus Rhyl whilst on vacation
Shovelled shit in Barrow
Appended drinks in Harrow
Lost my cherry in Londonderry To
a diamond cockney sparrow
Apprehended in Crewe
Cautioned on the Bakerloo
Incarcerated vagrancy Stockton on Tees
Last seen on a chain gang in the Florida Keys

Jesus wants me for a sunbeam
Heathen through and through
Refuse to prune the harvest flowers
Nor perch upon a Pugh
Doesn't make me nasty
Would give you a bite of my penultimate pasty
Non Christianity kindness affection
Many a good heart in the non-believer section

To smash the perfect omelette
Two dozen eggs should do
Then tip the contents into a pan
Until it turns to glue
Grated cheese wafer ham
Peppered sneezes
Damson jam
Present with chard
Stilton lingers
Season to taste
And dead man's fingers

Machete's clubs and Sherman Tanks
Murderer's dealer's dependants and skanks
Welcome to my former existence in a squat
Bullet wounds, syringes, a Borstal dot
Imposing deposing unforgiving and fierce
Shared a divan with a bloke from Milan Who
looked like Stuart Pearce!
Got out alive and started to thrive
Commenced a position at half past five
Will always enlighten
My heady days in Brighton
The squat may surprise and terrorise
The squat will always frighten

Life in the slammer
Nowt like nowt before
Bars on the windows
Iron for a door
All clanked shut
Slashed wrists head butt
Screw built like a shithouse rock
Pool balls swinging in a rancid sock
Though my crime was considered minimal
Now a lifelong hardened criminal
Slashing wrists dismembered grass
Virgins slammed up the Khyber Pass
Word of warning if never been
Be a good boy and keep your nose clean

Stuck in a lift
No need to panic
All I have to do is call the mechanic
Breathing affected
Panel disconnected
Malfunction disassemble provisionally detected
I cry for help
No help came
So I pooed myself again
Don't require a Coastguard
Nor your friendly local copper
Just a burly fireman with a reputable chopper
Can't locate the button for a merciful release
May curl up in a tiny ball and pass away in peace
Battled out of Alcatraz Vietnam and the Abyss
So why, oh why can't I get out of this
Difficult to comprehend
The end,

The ghost of dog through dusty stairs
A monkey missing one listens one glares
Whilst prying eyes from corners creep
Unexplained movements from shadows deep
A cloud of smoke to form a wish
A lantern beams on frightened fish

The hole grows wide for mice to hide
The monkey appears; he's there; he cried
One never knew that thoughts so deep
Could merge in sync whilst I am asleep

As a boy, I played on swings
Kissed the girls and bounced on springs
Avoided school and became aloof
Pilfered lead off the town hall roof
Went to Borstal
Bunked off maths
Wandered down some scary paths
Jailed for Vagrancy Street and urchin
Always learning always searching
For what I'll simply never know
You mature you wise
You realise
You grow

Walking down a country road
On the way to God knows where
The mind adopts a heavy load
Of worry panic and care

How come I am built this way What
causes me to roam?
Through town and hamlet, one must stray
Five hundred miles from home

My parents, they were settled folk
Resided in the east
Sister Kate a real nice bloke
Became an ordained priest

Rich kids pass me by in cars
Smile as if to say
There goes another wandering star
Survives from day to day

Tonight whilst wealthy lounge in bars
Surely I shall be
Somewhere residing under the stars
Propped up against a tree

Yes I'll keep on drifting
Until the day I die
Observing red sun lifting
Whilst the moon shines from the sky

Bought myself a curry
Love the stuff to bits
Only drawback being I always end up with the shits
Purchased close to Hastings
North West of The Ridge
Thank one's lucky stars I put a bog roll in the fridge.

Stood on a snail
Heard the shell crack
Poor little bugger had a mortgage on its back
Nice with garlic butter
A pricey glass of port
Now squashed on the pavement had a family to support
Should I arrange a funeral
Inform the next of kin So I
wrapped it in a betting slip
And chucked it in the bin.

When you are fat
Your flab is a ridge
When you are fat
You sit near the fridge
When you are fat you ditch the Coke Zero
When you are fat Hattie Jacques is your hero
When you are fat heathens mock the afflicted
All you can eat buffet's shamed and evicted
When you are fat you eat things at the fair
When you are fat you go straight through a chair
I was that fat bastard
Many kilos and more
Thankfully now I can fit through the door.

Hunt for seashells catch a crab
Burn your feet on a sandy slab
Pasta bowls Knickerbocker Glory
Kids re-enacting Jackanory
Sink in mud at lowest tide
Tickle a mollusc you decide
Beyond the harbour heading east
Discover a kiosk; indulge in a feast
Lick your ice cream grab a tea
Rent a beach hut by the sea
Explore the gifts the locals make
Stop to purchase home-made cake
A heritage of expectation
Discovered in the Lifeboat station
Welcome to Scarborough
Seen to be believed
A coastal gem where I was conceived.

Total moronic indignation
Life-enhancing medication
Tuesday couldn't get much nicer
Watching Morrison's bacon slicer
Allowing me to introduce Bexhill on Sea
Fuck all for breakfast nothing for tea
No British Home Stores John Menzies nor The Range
Highlight of the week is when the traffic lights change
No Stevie Wondering to Dance Yourself Dizzy
Stick a corpse in a bus stop and make the place busy
With an average age of five scores and twenty-two
There ain't an awful lot to do
Barricade the library
Drown in the sea
Arrange a mobility Sussex grand prix
There for the grace of God go I
Yorkshire till I die

Are you going to the Scarborough Fair?
Used to meet my school friends there
Bottle tops for Bingo
Coconuts were shy
European lingo
The goldfish couldn't fly
Dodgems crashing old men flashing
All the fun of the fair
Babies crying as onions fry
Two pounds twenty-five for a mince and onion pie
Excitement lights up the William Street sky
Dive bombers flying way up high
Throwing up on passers-by
Scream if ya wanna go faster
Ghost Train if ya dare
Are you going to the Scarborough Fair?

A man approaching 60
With traits of OCD
Little time for Germans
Passed away at 53
Don't like funeral parties
The veils that hide their faces
Issue travel permits
On a weekly daily basis
Feed the ducks in Barnet
Echoes down my chest
Impersonate Alf Garnet
In a pink fluorescent vest
My one undone ambition
For what it's worth to say
To bring back prohibition
On the outskirts of LA

If me mam had seen me homeless
Her heart would miss a beat
To see her oh sweet child of mine
A vagrant on the street
I never scrubbed a tide mark
Nor washed behind my snout
Oh to see the family baby
Down and almost out
She'd attempt to give me money
And inform me I was thin
Hang my head in shame
Whilst I was scoffing from a bin
My son he don't belong here
There must be some mistake
Why consuming bird seed
And a mouldy piece of cake
We all remain an inch away
From existing in this gruesome way
One false move one bad decision
And relegation to the third Division
Hope she's being looked after
In the Scarborough bit of heaven
Get the veg on mother
I'll be home just after seven

Oh so close to sixty
And what have I done
Slept in shop doorway's shot with a gun
Witnessed a murder drunk in West Ham,
Only to discover me sister's a man
Munich Interpol apprehending
Crimewatch appearance patent pending
Smashed every crevice
From bottom to top
Married a Cockerney
Forked out for a slut
Mastered the stopwatch in a knocking shop
Fenced for a tea leaf incarceration
Lost me front teeth Kangaroo interrogation
Transferred to chokey for cross-examination
How is he still with us
The inquisitive hollers
One lucky duck run like fuck And a
fistful of counterfeit dollars.

Once met a gangster in
Nottingham Station
A person who thrived on intense
confrontation
He asked for a whisky
And two shots of honey
I duly obliged coz he looked at me
funny
Tough somewhat threatening
but weak through and through
Behind that persona was
Me there was you
We all act as tough guys
But pendulums swing
I stood up to a man
Who stood down as a king

Whilst viewing
Gardner's World one day
A thought Occurred to
me Why don't I nip outside?
And purchase
Gammon ham for tea
Makes a change from roughage
Some chick peas
And a stew
Just to spice things up
Obtained my Haslet from Peru
Susan laid the table
Prepared some Mother's Pride
Just as I cured some extra matured
Black pudding on the side
All in all a roaring success
Despite a tiny spillage
Of Manuka on her dress
Proving beyond reasonable just what
Can be created
With a shovel full of parsley
And some ketchup Freshly grated!

Nowhere to run to
Nowhere to roam
I want to go home
Dementia

Clear and present danger
Familiarity
A dangerous stranger
Dementia

Displaying vulgarity
In uncharacteristic surroundings
Of extreme Familiarity
Dementia

General consensus
Away with the fairies
Never wait up for the crested canaries
Dementia

Repeating the same story
Of childhood wartime
Through guts and glory
Dementia

Gone that huge adventure
Discussing life
With an imaginary denture
Dementia

As the good Lord hands out pity
The Angels grant you peace
A merciful release
Dementia

The day we drove to Gateshead
Our hamster was on heat
Mother took the train
Because my dad had smelly feet
Our friendly local taxman
Gunning for a kill
Impounded our belongings
As we shot down Muswell Hill
The jolly home was hazardous
Pedal power by far
Primarily coz we didn't have
An engine in the car
Moral of this story
Yonder side is far from sunny
Especially when some
Jumped up little pip squeak
Wants your money.

Been in some tough situations
Begging for food on a bus
Drastic and rough confrontations
Big Issue, so desperate are us

I've pilfered grub from dustbins
Requested spare change on the street
Broke into hostelry larder's
Looking peaky with nothing to eat

Slurped packet soup from a kitchen
With regulation one slice of bread
Prescribed special cream for the itching
With a yearning to wake up whilst dead

Witnessed a murder
Moved on by the law
Favours for money
Slept on a floor

Found a job whilst destitute
Climbed another rung
Refused to rot
Snuck in a squat
My redemption song had finally sung

Life on the streets isn't easy
Frowned on by nasty and bar
Abused by affluent morons
No matter how desperate you are

My best friend has a cancer diagnosis
Biopsy scan conclusive prognosis
Bad it has affected me
Known each other since we were three

Conker string football card
Playing out in me mam's back yard
Though maintaining a sense of frivolity
Inevitable bouts of endless radiology

Through life's great highway, we drifted apart
Together forever and never to part
Till socials brought us back together
To a future filled with stormy weather

Needles tablets chemo and pill
Never thought he would get So ill
Tubes and liquids opiate cream
Are things all bad as they seldom seem

He'll keep on fighting as Vikings do
Made of sterner stuff than you
As a friend, I'll monitor the condition
Until his torso screams remission

A tricky old subject
Taboo to the masses
Just what occurs
When somebody passes
Do we fry or do we burn
Is it me inside
The cylindrical urn
Ashes to Ashes
Lively to still
Anybody I know
They are reading the will
Wrapped in a shroud
Plus three layers of bedding
First time he's been stiff Since
the night of the wedding
For those left behind
Things can be rough
We all have to die If
we live long enough.

With prices at an all-time high
And natives getting tense
Can't believe a lettuce head
Costs much more than fifty pence

Nice to recall when fresh air was free
Especially in Abergavenny
Cycling home for me chippy tea
Coz haddocks were twenty-a-penny

Oh for a time machine
Transport me back
To where I've been
When laughter was a snigger
And Kit Kats were much bigger

So there we are
The sands of time
Indifferent era into rhyme
Challenging stairways we must climb

Will things get any better
Will I stop sounding hoarse
Will I relocate to Finland Second
class of course.

My dinner list is simple
This dining list is long
My dinner list is up for sale
And going for a song

Would choose to share my nibbles
With Bandy Bert from Crewe
A selection of migration nuts
Wrapped in a rabbit stew

Starter would be Albert Carter
Brainchild of the People's Charter
Oyster Pearl's on rocket leaves
Surrounded by Police and thieves

Main course a rather jolly affair
Every cast member from Vanity Fair
Marinated tofu primarily raw
Enough to paralyse any man's jaw

Desert a choice of Creosote and figs
Moccacino with hints of parts from pigs
After dinner mints and snuff
Devoured by Pele and Brian Clough.

A man who is homeless forgoes all his pride
No means or where with all to spend a night inside
Friends are non-existent
Shoulder has a chip
Locals are insistent
That his clothes come from a skip
Days are nothing different
In a spiral of confusion
Lamb and mutton stew simply
An optical illusion
A kaleidoscope of doubt
Within a nightmare of delusion
Streets that he wanders
Paved with indecision
Rife with animosity
Prejudice and derision
Until the good Lord takes him
Or an angel mops his brow
Somebody up there likes him Doing
better now!

Whilst still down and almost out
A pub man said to me
Will you come and pull my pints
From eight till half past three
In a charming Southern hamlet
Namely Brighton
By the sea
Dossing in a car park
The drill was not to shirk
Attempt to look presentable
And get yourself to work
Pub in question lacked some charm
With sawdust on the floor
Came face to face with knuckles
When he gracefully flew
Directly through
The Ladies' shithouse door
As I settled into things
This barman was for hire
The locals really warmed to me
They set the place on fire
Regular riots
Black eyes and a bruise
Even the arms on the chairs had tattoos
Eventually on to pastures better
Kept in touch with friends gone by
Via prison visit and a reminiscent
letter!

When I was a little boy
My home it was my manor
If someone tried to steal my ball
I hit them with a hammer
Behind us was a coal yard
Supervised by Stan
Who kept our houses
Nice and warm
In the winter with his van
Mr Raine sold bicycles
My bike he sold to mum
And every time
I pulled a brake
The seat went up
Me bum

A tiny dog went fishing
His name was simple Sam
All he caught was Influenza
3 bananas and a pram
He didn't have equipment
Just a back pack
And some string
Felt sorry for the
Little ones because
They couldn't swim
So he issued them with
Armbands
And threw them straight back in
Expecting salmon hake
And huss
An ornamental London Bus
His mind began to lingers
All he got was potted shrimp
And a box of cheap fish fingers

Why does it always rain
When will the sun come back again
My fulcrum ties in knots and muddles
As I dodge a path through all the puddles
A soaking coat a cheap umbrella
An optimistic paper seller
Water limit substantially breached
End of my tether unanimously reached
Buckets to empty things went through
As a cruise liner sails up the M62

We pray for a lull
We yearn for subsidence
We ask for the experts
To give us some guidance
So until the clouds are empty
Whilst staying just afloat
I'll sail up to the stars
In a self-constructed boat

Noises are annoying
Noises can be loud
From exited auctioneers
To a raucous football crowd
Noises are infectious
Noises make a sound
Noises can be deafening
When the mother-in-law pops round
Noises in the workplace
Crashes thuds and dins
Noises when the council men
Are emptying the bins
Dulcet tones hand-held phones
Agitation level slightly
Should one intend to make a row
Please do so very quietly

The day I had my tonsils out
They weren't half bloody sore
Precisely why the surgeon
Held me two feet off the floor
It wasn't tonsillitis
It wasn't Asian Flu
It was a touch debilitating
As I couldn't tie my shoe
He used a heavy implement
Some scissors and a wrench
As the blood flowed uncontrollably
On a cushioned marble bench
As I staggered out of theatre
A nation breathed a sigh
Tucking into haslet
And a homemade apple pie
Leaving through the Mortuary door
My bodily function was no more
Found some time to look around
To check being alive was safe and sound
I'm a homeless man at Christmas
It isn't quite my time
Won't be under Mistletoe
Nor guzzling mulled wine
Won't be with a long lost friend
No driving grandma round the bend

I'm a homeless man at Christmas
For all the world to see
Won't be singing carols
Or watching Charles at three
Have a hunch be soup for festive lunch
Ode to the dreaded crouton crunch

I'm a homeless man at Christmas
Yearning to compete
With anti-social revellers
In a decomposing street
One Bedsit plus a begging bowl
My life would be complete

I'm a homeless man at Christmas
Empty doorway was my stable
Plus a giant Rediffusion box
Discovered near a table
No midget gems no brand-new socks
Define this tragic fable

I'm a homeless man at Christmas
So only I shall know
What it's like to beg for money
Whilst freezing in the snow
Dream of others drunk at parties
As I open up some stolen Smarties

I'm a homeless man at Christmas
Heading for a fall
From the bottom of my empty bag
Merry Christmas to you all
Please spare a thought for hunger pain
As you stumble past me in the rain

A dreaded low-carb diet
Two cake shelves and a ghost
You crave for chicken korma
Sugared almond beans on toast

Mrs Pugh from twenty-two
Obtained a gastric band
Last seen in the hot dog queue
With a burger in her hand

A genuine consensus
No easy task to undertake
"Can I have some Scampi fries Or a lemon drizzle cake"

The dreaded weekly weigh-in
Hope and optimism fails
As poor Mrs Hansen
Collapsed the bathroom scales

A lifelong search for wafer ham
And salad should be plenty
Drop a size for Christmas
Getting down to just a twenty

Through years of good intention
She bought a yoga mat
It's just water retention
Sod the diet, staying fat

Amazing gear is bog roll
The secret is to poo it
Purchase a cheap one
You put your finger through it
Essence of sandpaper
Doesn't make things easier
Scrape it once too often
And some skin leaves your posterior
The dearer stuff is softer
With a picture of a dog
Doesn't hide the fact
We spend an hour on the bog
The moral of this story
Without causing any harm
When on the loo
Don't let the poo
Go halfway up your arm
Whilst walking back from Crewe one day
A thought occurred to me
If it's Christmas in Mombasa
It's only half past three
Why does the wasp
When does the bee
How does the wasp
Sit down to have his tea
If you talk to an Eskimo
His breath will freeze your ear
When it's night time in Italy
It's Wednesday over here

From bats in the belfry
To shadows on the wall
Cats in the cradle
To tremors in the hall
Why 'tis the witching season
Front Perth to Inverness
Giving every reason
To be Frightened half to death
Ouija boards are nervous
Mediums are wary
Spiders crawl back in their Web
And find it very scary
With consecrated floorboards
And things inside a jar
Spirits lurking on the stairs
Behind the servants' bar
Exorcism Central
Enter if you dare
Now Bagdale Hall is up to rent
Coz nobody wants to live there

'

Endured some crazy mishaps
Since arriving out to dock
Head first in a duck pond
Swallowed the winder off the clock
Straight through a plate glass window
Dragged Behind a bus
Shopping trolley mayhem
With the minimum of fuss
I was a human cannonball
Which didn't go so well at all
A pregnant bullock broke my fall
Adjacent to The Albert Hall
Swallowed by a killer whale
Spat at by a giant snail
Choked to death on Curly kale
And lived to tell the tale

My mum and dad
Were past it
When I shot right
Into view
She was only thirty-nine
He was fifty-two
Whipped his thing out
Far too late
It was a genuine mistake
Raising baby
Caused quite a fix
So they locked me in a cupboard
Until I was six
Collecting me from Primary School
Was far from something canny
Assuming he was grandad
And mother was my granny
Flat caps war tales
Vera Lynn and lotion
When all I craved was Oxford bags And a dance to Billy Ocean
As I got older stuff got worse
When Mother couldn't find her purse
Then father slowly Lost the plot
Which jeopardised
His borstal dot
Game set and match
To Lendl and Connors
They passed away quite peacefully
With full military honours

I used to be a machine
Factory kept me nice and clean
Churned out letterheads of green
I used to be a machine

I used to be a tramp
Sleeping out in places damp
Two crunchies and a Lava lamp
I used to be a tramp

I used to be some slime
Staining things from time to time
Envisaging a life of crime
I used to be some slime

I used to be a beam
Complete with a hyperactive gleam
Prison walls a distant dream
I used to be a beam

I used to have a stammer
Couldn't pronounce a run down town in Alabama
A section 15 and a month in the slammer
I used to have a stammer

I used to have a dream
Of being Mr Big on the corporate scene
Selected pastimes most obscene
I used to have a dream

I used to be a bell
But now my life can go to hell
Once a torso now a shell
I used to be a bell

The street was getting hotter
As inferno filled the air
People were distracted
On their way to Scarborough Fair
Everyone was looking
Thought it was the
Hot dogs cooking
People crying onions frying
Any prize ya like
Atmosphere seemed mellow
'Coz the sky was
Turning yellow
Sirens thundered through
The town
As everything was
Burning down
All because a little boy
Set fire to his sister's toy
Recently fostered
From war-torn Romania
Received six months For Pyromania
No mention in dispatches
As children shouldn't
Play with matches

As suicidal tendencies
Encapsulate your mind
Spare a thought
For loved ones
For those who are left behind
Spare a thought for heartache
And staring at the door
Left with only memories
Of a life you had before
Picking up the pieces
Existence filled with hope
Eighteen years of matrimony
Dangling from a rope
I was that person
Back in the day
The only thing I have to say
It doesn't have to be that way

Dropping a dress size for Christmas
I really don't know what to do
Double up on the asparagus
Or urinate in the ragout
Difficult to discover your gastronomic niche
Whilst munching upon a freshly baked quiche
Buy some salad crack a smile
Go out walking for a while
Eliminate pasta; incorporate fish
Utilize a smaller dish
No need to panic
Or chew on a leek
Coz my diet always starts next week

Me Dad's friend Dickie Mennell
Only had one leg
Other just a peg
Worked the Hispaniola, seasonal troubled strife
Never paid for a single shoe in his car crash of a life
Married long time beau called Pat
Who made a living on her back
Long John Silver doppelganger
Who's hip flask made him shout and shiver
Any lip from children
Dispatched them in the river
Oh the Perils of the sea
Backhanders Insults predominantly
free
As he hopped his way to immortality
Season ended
Eye patch nearly mended
Bedsit Destitution
As the good Lord intended
A working-class hero
Shown a poverty-stricken door
They don't make people
Like him anymore
Cry for help Munchausen injections
Representation unreliable intentions
Funeral for a pauper
No trainee pirate stopped for a while
For this jolly Jack Tar character who
made the children smile.

People may not like my style
From shelling crabs in Ventnor
To hovels in Carlisle
Many year's spent on the road
Eye of a bat and wing of toad
Filey bore the brunt of me
As did Durrington on Sea
Scarborough people, not so keen
Precisely why I fled the scene
With Scampi fries and Sour cream
Kent it pulled out all the stops
To get me gone they called the cops
Should've kept their noses clean
And stuck to picking hops
Life's essential misfit
Everywhere I go
Left to my own devices
Making pissholes in the snow

Tried the art of jogging
A body needs to be mended
Cholesterol was a cricket score A
waist severely extended

Reached the private Gasworks
Close to Holbeck Hill
Lactic acid gripped me
With my fetlocks very ill

With the pace slowing, discomfort growing
Decided to go for the burn
Cheeks were glowing cock's were crowing
As snail Overtook on the bend of a turn

Racked in pain
Felt like I'd never steam rhubarb again
Lungs a bursting angina attack
Managed to get to Home Bargains and back

Eventually cracked it through wars of Attrition's
A solitary figure enduring adverse conditions
Numerous eccentrics endure the test
Of righting all wrongs in a white running vest

My wife has also got the bug
Athletics is upon her
Every time a bang goes off
She does a lap of honour

Olympic Games will never be
Running is my saviour
Commitment some will never see
In persona and general behaviour

Someone's daughter
Someone's son
Battered spouses on the run
Tales of sadness tales of woe
Tales of nowhere else to go
Shelter in a library
Sit under a tree
Time is not an issue
As you crave a pot of tea
Your picture in newspapers
But homeless is no fun
Somebody's daughter
Somebody's son

When I was homeless hurt me mouth
Unlucky scenario for North man down South
Didn't have cash
For a treatment transaction
Nor rusty tools
For a street-based extraction
Went to the practice
Would they take a shilling
To tidy up me molar
And knock me up a filling
With the minimum of drilling
Snotty bird behind the desk
The archetypal honey
Did somewhat detest
My unusual request
Of settling my account with not much money
Ejected still in agony
With a pain down to me spleen
Failed to leave heartbroken
Coz I Pinched a magazine
Taxied to a local pub
With toothache mumps and gout
Upset the local football thug
Who knocked the thing clean out
Forgot to write and thank him
As he struggles with a stammer
Currently incarcerated
In a reputable slammer
So there u have my story
Of oral guts and glory
Experts have provisionally agreed
To knock it out on Jackanory.

Good morning all the homeless
How are you today
Hope you've brushed your teeth
And put the cardboard box away

Breakfast time approaches
Destitution in a tin
Abhorrently nutritious
From the nearest wheelie bin

Strangers give you money
Yet glare back in disdain
At this repulsive little creature
Begging in the pouring rain

As wintertime bares down on us
Survival can be rare For one
forgotten hero And a world
that doesn't care.

Methadone and beer
One lethal combination
Is no apparent reason
For a street-life situation

Some survive with the Salvation Army
Vitamin pills and Chilli con carne Johnny came
home to a hero's reception
Hasn't been seen since absconding to
Wrexham.

Next time you go shopping
Be sure to search for deals
Bogof rum and raisin
Half-price jellied eels

Don't forget the bargain bin
For stuff that can't be sold
A badly bashed-up tuna tin
Plus stilton caked in mould

Nice delights down every aisle
To stave the hunger for a while
Eccles cakes, a chocolate log
Some smelly stuff to clean the bog

Onto produce if I do
Plenty for that hearty stew
Sweet potatoes dates and spuds
Ideal for wraps and Yorkshire puds

So there we are the weekly shop
Fill that trolley till we drop
Please save a pound for one last flutter
With that lady at the lottery shutter

My so much vaunted schooldays
Detention was a must
Spider eyes and Mouse's thighs
In Julie Harper's pizza crust

Exam fails various sales
Knock off jars of honey
Anecdotes and naughty tails
Of Stealing people's money

Claimed the back seat of the bus
Front of every queue
Made the staff room hall of fame
For pissing in the stew

Left the place with nothing
They said I had potential
Where Sally Beet from Craven Street
Now works for the Prudential

A gentle word of warning
Try not to act the fool
Bright days will be dawning
If you knuckle down at school

When will this world stop fighting
Why can't we love each other
Why can't we show compassion
To our sister and our brother

Why does the world cite conflict?
Why do we launch attack?
Why can't we find the where with all
To love each other back

Why do we not feel safer?
When we close our own front door
Why do we Bury loved one's
Through casualties of war

Why won't the world stop turning
If cease-fire can't be found
A thought inside is burning
A wish it wasn't round
And so it will continue
From Ukraine to Timbuktu
A slaughter of the innocent
What have they done to you?

Whilst peering at a constellation
My life came under scrutinization
Bouts of severe condemnation
From suits in higher Authorisation
Steeped in heavy dramatization
With occasional sniffs of constipation
Have caused unbridled aggravation
From Milton Keynes to Reading station
Jobless for an occupation
With very little education
Sleep deprivation
Born out of prescribed prescription psychotic medication
Alfresco accommodation
Slight tendency for an altercation
A menace to the population
One too many confrontation
Inevitable incarceration
Now receiving adulation
As I wave goodbye to infestation
So reciting this short dissertation
'Tis never too late for acclamation
So buckle up this once-great nation
Fingers up at gesticulation
Have a very nice vacation
Some sangria and fornication
Whilst you rise in people's estimation

Close enough to Filey
Not near to Camden Town
Locals were informed
To put their head upside down

A local man went missing
Until he had been found
Seemed the obvious way
To keep an ear to the ground

My mouth was on my forehead
My eyes were on my gum
My nostrils facing skywards
So the mucus didn't run

Looking upwards to the floor
Sun and sky are all I saw
Would our victim cry out loud
As I wandered lonely on a cloud

The bloke from number forty-three
Was warned he must behave
Stubble on a makeshift head
So chanced a cheeky shave

Eventually, a man was found
Nose on backwards safe and sound
Head's reshaped put through a mangle
Though some still at an awkward angle

Diary of a Northern man
Subtle hints of Desperate Dan
Awaiting Frank the pastry man With
extra in the griddle pan

Gurgle's with carbolic
Naughty bits in Vim
Crack and sack with Kitchen Flash From
glory hole to rim

The local population
In fear of foot and mouth
How could this uncouth creation Relocate down south

Vodka on his Cornflakes
Creosote in his tea
Choking on their cupcakes
In Laa de Daa on Sea

He Insults all the neighbours
Repulsiveness and smut
Is this the man God gave us Knotted
hanky beer gut

A local pompous happy band
Who investigates malaria
Unfair tactics underhand
To eject him from the area

And so shall it continue
This regional divide
Hail to our neanderthal
With a ferret by his side.

A gypsy went to Camden Lock
To peddle all his ware's
A welly boot a bandicoot
And quirky things for chairs

He didn't have a table
So put stuff on the floor
A portrait of Tom Courtney
Plus a blow torch made of straw

The London population
Were sceptical at best
At this travelling connotation
With medals on his chest

Sales were hitting record highs
Bits going for a song
Till a man with Bette Davis eyes
Was sent to move him on

Settling in Maida Vale
This man's whole life was up for sale
Tea lights hand kites buttons and stone
A life-size statue of Sylvester Stallone

Eventually, he flogged the lot
Including Granny's Borstal dot
Last seen preaching constipation
Adjacent to a Polling Station

Opened a window and influenza
Didn't see it coming
My head is sore my throat is raw
My follicles shake, my nose is running

Doctor prescribed cylindrical spheres
For under me tongue and right down me ears
Plenty of fluids some bed rest and butter
Now I walk with a sniffle and talk with a stutter

Torpedo Suppositories next stuff to come
Out of a box and Straight up me bum
True as an arrow my aim was complete
As discharge flew out seven blocks up the street

Powders creams inhalers and snuff
Milk of Magnesia is not quite enough
To cure this man of diagnostic flu
A veterinary surgeon from a reputable zoo

Ruled out distemper hard pad and fleas
Every time I broke a nail me chest began to wheeze
Failed to discard terminal no overall assurance
So I visited an undertaker and upped the insurance

Many things I don't like
Many things I do
Clearing leaves on a windy day
Pomegranate stew
Tiddlywinks with a lifelong friend
Changing trains at Elmers End
History of the Cutty Sark
Cogitating in the dark
Acquaintances in higher places
Corporate stuff at Ascot races
Like or loathe shall I confess
Perhaps an educated guess
But I don't like mess

Father was an evil man
Walloped me mam with an omelette pan
Threw us in the house back yard
Never sent a birthday card
A drunken pig devoid of morals
Festering all day in Corals
Never put his family first
Through Bigamy and raging thirst
Spoke with his Fists
Answered with obscenities
One paternal barrage
Of Insults and extremities
Never kicked a ball about
'Coz all he did was scream and shout
Woodbines in a dirty vest
A girl in every Bedsit nest
My old mum really was the best
Until one June in eighty-eight
Not a day too
late
Nobody cried, he
Died

I've had employment Issues
Recycling snotty tissues
Placing things in thingy me bobs
Constructing corn for kernel cobs
From unwanted abject object demolisher
To conscientious black pudding polisher
Hung up hats hung up coats
Titillated empty fishing boats
Keep your pride in menial graft
With no specific specialist craft
Refuse collection dustcart inspection
Accompanied pigs for truffle detection
All in a day
For an antidote taster
From no good at school
To society waster

Cataclysmic nonsense
A supernatural force
People chasing battery hens
Two buckets for the horse
Scoop it tie it bag it and bin it
Anything with Margaret Lockwood in it Three
cheers for Albert Hargreaves
Plus Aubergine for lent
Please don't pay the ferryman 'Coz I owe him 3 weeks rent.

First time I went to London
Was quite the culture shock
No pies on the menu
No pit boots with a frock
Not much sense of humour
Beer flat and weak
Everyone talks funny Cockney
Quirky yet unique
Pie and mash with snotty sauce
Funny eels in jelly
Cabs for hire to Buckinghamshire
People off the telly
From Gardens Kew to London Zoo
Is always quite a lot to do
Midnight feast will do just fine
Then home along the District line
Jump a Bus to Hampstead
A train to Bethnal Green
Waxing lyrical Madam Tussauds
England batting first at Lords
Vertigo diagnosis not recommended
A trembling torso highly suspended
Travelling Swiftly up the Shard
Changing of the guard
They don't like us we don't like them
From Heckmondwike to News at Ten
Civil war shall always roam
If only Brentford were at home
As we gaze across the London Eye
One craves a steak and kidney pie
Without much time for condemnation
From King's Cross back to Seamer station

I am but a simple man
From common blocks of streets
A fondness for suburbia
With a love for buttered sweets
Never asked to be here
Didn't choose my name
Don't do histrionics
Travel everywhere by train
Mother was a dental nurse
Father was a fool
Sister was a lunatic
Who dragged a box to school
Academically I failed my test
Couldn't get past zero
Busy watching Georgie Best
Who was my childhood hero
Never been to Gretna Green
Never learnt to bleat
From darkest Cheam to seldom seen
My boots are full of feet
Life sure can be fickle
Reputations fall from grace
As a momentary trickle
Cascades upon my face
Manipulation central
From Brixham to Gibraltar
Should I do it all again
My chakra has to alter
Will carry on revolving
No other choice to make
Until this world stops turning
Am just one huge mistake

Females at home parties
With two nods and a wink
Can overdose on Smarties
And throw up in the sink

A kitchen congregation
Occurs at every call
Whilst mine host is distracted
Having sex against the wall

Invited patrons only
Plus gatecrashers's and more
The lame the sick the lonely
Spilling discharge on the floor

House is slowly crumbling
As the boys begin to flirt
Stereo goes tumbling
With a carpet badly hurt

Into the witching hour
Whilst listening to Mark Bolan
Many stair rods are removed
And ornaments are stolen

No More crazy parties
Just as it came to pass
The dog was doused in shaving gel
And the windows had no glass

With mum and dad expected back
Jack superglued to the chimney stack
No place for the mild or meek
'Cos there's another one next week

Since I was conceived
Many injuries received
Breakages numerous fractures three
Bruising round the humorous and a brand new spanking knee
Nuts screws buttons and bows
Hold stuff together from my head to my toes
Broke my back in many regions
Affecting some homoeopathic legions
Extensive prognosis required a taxi
Plus a camera up me jacksy
The fact I still exist is an amazement in itself
As half my body parts are gently pickling on a shelf
Broke my wrist broke my arm
Popped a boil watching Emmerdale
Farm
My jaw clicks my eyes twitch
My ears pop my teeth itch
If life expectancy was a factor to remember
Should've been dead come September.

If you've ever hitched a lift somewhere
You understand my tales
Attempt snotty Sussex
From near the Yorkshire Dales
First, you need a thumb
And a passenger seat manner
A copy of The Times
Plus a where you going banner
Picked up very quickly
By a man in trendy gear
Dropped me off at Wakefield
In his Vauxhall Cavalier
Next a posh convertible
With driver true to type
Female vacuum salesman
Who smoked a chimney pipe
Took me close to Mansfield
Near sixteen bales of hay
Was I on the road to hell
Or the road to Mandalay
Many days later
After several ups and downs
Not far from the Equator
Some cities and some towns
My head down in an airfield
A run-in with the law
Two dozen Fiat Punto's
And a slot on Channel four
Arrived in sunny Brighton
Five minutes from the station
Big congratulations sir
You have reached your destination

Why can't our world be happy?
Why are we all so sore?
Why can't we crack a smile when someone Lets
us through a door?
Why can't we like a food bank
Spare a fire for the log
Why can't we feed the homeless
When our streets are filled with fog
Why do we look for trouble
Why do we scowl and moan
Why don't we champion optimism
Or give the dog a bone
Why don't we give to charity
Nor man a raffle stall
Why were we born so miserable
Why were we born at all

Often think of what I did
When nothing more than just a kid
Lager peanuts rum and lust
As another brain cell bit the dust

What became of this human clone
Yorkshire's answer to Al Capone
Addicted to many bad pariahs
Sniffing glue and black maria's

Barred from every pub in town
For pulling ladies' trousers down
Fought a fight and fight the fought
Regularly up in court

For dodgy dealings, he's your man
Straight bananas hot dog van
Shares in ninety-eighty-three
No money back no guarantee

A light it shone upon me
A beacon from above
Was all this bad boy needed
Incentive and a shove

You may well have deciphered
That reprobate was me
Now working as a laundromat
In Redemption by the Sea.

Define a pet hate
Perhaps it's too late
Children swinging on a rusty gate
Black bananas standing in queues
When Tottenham Hotspur unexpectedly lose
Nothing at bingo small sausage rolls
Can't speak the lingo
For whom the bell tolls
Average at chess
Bandwagon stress
Going to School in a sparkly dress
Lying politicians
Warring ammunitions
People on Skateboards
Eating competitions
Pineapple pizza
A tortoiseshell coat
Right gives me the
goat

Why do rich people buy themselves out of the equation
Of mixing with the folk of a low denomination
How can affluence justify
A man scraping mould from a rancid pork
Pie
Corporate banking up in the air
Scowling at the needy on a wing and a prayer
Saville Row pin stripes
Brolly and bowler
Utterly oblivious to a street urchin stroller
All we desire is pity and compassion
In a dog-eat-dog world where survival is on ration.

A day at the races
And what do we see
Shed loads of interest
In horse number three
Jockey on board is a really good driver
Guaranteed profit
For only a fiver
Up go the traps
As they romp down the track
Our flying machine
Is right at the back
Approaching the finish
We let out a gasp
The four-legged wonder
Has finished stone last
Hang on to your money
Be frugal my friend
The bookmaker always Succeeds
in the end.

The homeless man
He carries the can
A roach, a match, a tissue
A twenty-eight-day nuisance ban
For selling The Big Issue
He doesn't know what day it is
As he whistles in the rain
A human water closet
Who forgot to pull the chain
The doorway is a haven
In which to share his dreams
Of a life now desiccated
And broken at the seams
He steals a tuna sandwich
In Vegan wholemeal bread
Pondering the drawbacks
Of a future without a bed
An ideal plan
In a mixed-up head
Perhaps someday he'll wake up dead

A very tetchy subject
Referred to as Taboo
Chocolate brown in colour
That sticky stuff called poo

A bodily necessity
Of that, there is no doubt
A squeeze, a smile, a grimace
As we strain to get it out

Works its way through our Tubes
Performing loop the loop
Resembling a house brick
Or mother's oxtail soup

His majesty the King performs
As does the merchant navy
Gushing out in many forms
From clay to Bisto gravy

So in your home whilst on the throne
Recite some words and vowels
Because we need to concentrate
Whilst emptying our bowels

Now listen up you girls and boys
Said pastime not immune to noise
From King's Lynn to Seattle
In church or Chapel let it rattle.

A child Approaching Christmas
Is something we behold
Immense anticipation
Of stories to be told
Excitement etched on faces
As Rudolph steams ahead
To all the little people
Who are fast asleep in bed
Maisie eyes a Barbie Doll
Bobby wants a trowel
Dolly fancies anything
To do With Simon Cowell
Current destination
Ding dong merrily on high
Time for Harvey's Bristol Cream
And a piping hot mince pie
Snow is falling Santa's calling
Hearts are filled with glee
As everybody's presents
Are placed beneath the tree
Cometh the morning cometh the noise
Selection boxes mechanical toys
Mother under instant attack
Forgetting the batteries that slot in the back
As things calm down and foxes snore
Carol singers at the door
Brand new shoes fit brand new feet
Another Christmas Day complete
A festive time approaches
Expectation fills the air
Spare a thought for those in need
For those who Christ forgot to feed

When I was a little boy
I often broke the law
Destroying next door's mulberry Bush
With Grandad's circular saw
Never home for seven
Always on the Rob
If people disrespected me
I smacked them in the gob
Rumbled nicking rhubarb
Bombastic and uncouth
Pilfered clothes from washing lines
Stripped lead off every roof
With a growing fetish
For chip shop gherkins
Once cleared the shelves
At Dorothy Perkins
Concerned authorities at the door
'Coz at the time was only four
Just a stage he's going through
When I stole a pig from Whipsnade Zoo
No one knew quite what to do
Extradite him to Peru
Looking back in jest and fury
Yet to sit on a public jury
These days calm not wild but mellow
A rather chilled out amaiable fellow

A subject we debate about
Best to shut our mouth
Who's the better person
Northern versus South
Been going on for decades
In pubs on trains to Deal
We have Geoffrey Boycott
They have Kathy Beale
Who can shout the loudest
Drive the biggest car
Who can spot an Aardvark
In an igloo from afar
Our girls are prettier
Yours belch after pop
A Northern lass will purchase brass
In a haberdashery shop
A Southerner's perspective
Designer clothes and bling
A Northerner's objective
Always fart before you sing
Who's football team is better
Who helped to win the war
Who brews the strongest Beer
Does anyone know the Millwall score
They eat Caviar quails and jam
Employ a maid to support West Ham
We eat tripe scotch mist and spam
Reside in caves and hatch a plan
Actually, befriended a Southerner
Who sits at the end of my tether
Sometimes discuss the weather
Perhaps we could learn a skill together

Wish I didn't need to shave
Cosmetic fall from pristine grace
Strutting about with whiskers
Plastered all over my face

Twelve when spotted stubble
Whilst shopping in the town
Thought that someone else
Had put my head upside down

Cut myself to ribbons
From childhood to confusion
Required plastic surgery
Plus a second blood transfusion

Puberty and facial hair
Boy to manhood wasn't fair
Another thing I had to ship
That caterpillar on my lip

Often leave it for a week
Imposing shadows on my cheek
Went electric three days later
Buzzing like a whore's vibrator

A habit I'm not keen on
A habit always feared
Live life caked in toilet roll
Or grow a bushy beard.

A thinking man
Not a drinking man
Stuff would've so much changed
Wouldn't be a psychopath
Nor socially deranged
Never be spotty, nor silly or fat
Nor attempt to vomit on next-door's cat
Society would rejoice
Without the sound of my booming voice
Would've gone to college
Could've paid the rent
Given up the fraudulence
And burglary for lent
Opened up a juice bar
In Durrington on Sea
Joined the local women's guild
Had Chelsea buns for tea
Sadly never happen
Chose the dodgy door
Opted for destruction
Whilst unconscious on the floor

Password pin code Mother's maiden name
All items required to get you in the game
Postcode blood group, something made of tin
Please recite in Japanese or you ain't getting in
Account has been locked
Company denies
Details blocked
Too many tries
Please log in and go online at your leisure
Because messing you about has been an absolute pleasure
Payment denied attempt not to scoff
Our sound advice for you is to send a pigeon off.

As I was outside jogging
A mouse appeared beside
He clambered on my footwear
And hitched a little ride
He sat there very quietly
Without uttering a squeak
Only to explain
He will be here again next week
Eventually alighting
He left without a fuss
Whispering so sweetly
That he'd gone and missed the bus

In the land of funny elephants
Everybody smiles
Nobody is miserable for miles and miles and miles
They sleep in big pyjamas
Have broken all the bunks
Eat thousands of bananas
And tickle with their trunks
Everything is jolly
In this jungle land of tricks
Bamboo shoots with honey
And a belly full of ticks
I hope to visit there one day
A splendid place in which to play
As tiny ones belie their fears
With playful grins and floppy ears.

A small frog knocked upon my door
His name was Jimmy Tickle
Licked my windows squeaky clean
Was such a lovely shade of green

He hopped into my living room
Made himself at home
Announced he was a vegan
And give the dog a bone

I asked if he was hungry
So offered him a snack
Prepared some peppered tofu
On a squashed tomato stack

He said he was an amphibian
Of which I was aware
Strangely then proceeded
To trim his nasal hair

He thanked my hospitality
And waved his magic wand
Proclaiming me most welcome
In a local lily pond

A very pleasant creature
Not rude nor brash nor fickle
Was privileged to be a wheel
In the cog of Jimmy Tickle

Am quite a pleasant person
Slippery when wet
Want to go to Ecuador
Haven't done it yet
Worshipped Desmond Lynam
Milked a Friesian bull
Opened up a trading post
In Kingston upon Hull
Keen on Herman's Hermits
Eggs and slip-on shoes
Never miss John Cooper Clarke
When mentioned on the news
Respectful of diversion
Philately and trust
Left stranded in suburbia
When Thomas Cook went bust
The object of this witty verse
Far from being a tad averse
To revel in my nonsense
Before it gets much worse.

Love a crisp
Disrupts my lisp
Devour them from mouth to hand
Any flavour
Any brand
Immerse the texture
Embrace the crunch
Cheese and onion
With my lunch
Purchase at the garage
Chuck 'em in a flan
Enjoy some in a sandwich
If it isn't breaded ham
Soggy for a casserole
Excellent on toast
Chill beef and mustard
Are the ones I like the most
Eat them in pyjamas
Scoff them in my socks
Buy a pack of seven
Devour them by the box
My wedding breakfast had 'em
With Lea and Perrins sauce
With resulting acrimonious
Salt and vinegar divorce

Alfie is a chimpanzee
Drinks champagne and builder's tea
Working as a plumbers mate
In Bridlington somewhere on Sea

His bum is pink and shiny
A button nose, so cute
With fingers very tiny
Lives on potted meat and fruit

His mummy didn't want him
His daddy was a fool
He never had a dummy
And didn't go to school

Grew up very quickly
Checked out at the vet
Sold his toys on eBay
And bought a maisonette

Now residing comfortably
With money in the bank
He hangs out with a Pygmy goat
And drives a Sherman Tank

A local privy Councillor
He thrives on dissertation
Through after dinner speaking
On the monkey population

Moral of this fable
This quite amazing story
Bringing to his table
Many tales of guts and glory

Life can be brutal
Life can be bad
Things can be nasty
Things can be sad
Some Situations
Arrive at a cost
Souls can be empty
Hearts can be lost
Battle your demons
Confront your soul
Dig yourself out
Of a difficult hole
Never give up
Never repent
Someday your mind
Will be calm and content
Life can be brutal
Shout it out loud
Reach for the sunshine
And do us all proud

Popped out to see a medium Didn't catch his name
Insistent dear mother spent a lifetime on the game
Eyed no past or future
Didn't have a clue
Said my Auntie's cousin ran a brothel in Peru
Crossed his palm with silver
As he turned the other cheek
Failed to pick a winning horse at
Kempton Park next week
Said my dog ran market stalls
Unreliable lottery balls
His trance-like state gave a conversational sound
Miraculously me Father had recently been found
Reminding me I still owe him a pound
As I sat in amazement with doubts in my head
Entertaining a man who can talk to the dead
He cited a shed load of dosh in the tank
Acutely aware
As I'd just robbed a bank
Simply a conman or psychotically gifted
Just as my sanctum, my chakra had shifted
Such a transformation as his eyes began to roam
So I spoke to John F Kennedy
Then sauntered home alone

Stuck inside the queue of a reputable grocer
Cashier at the front isn't getting any closer
Only came along for some butter and a mop
Customers in front of me are buying half the shop
No person lets me through as my haul is only two
Standing here at will until I make it to the till
Why no common decency
Do we blame the war on Brexit
So I slam my money on the belt
And head straight for the exit.

When I had all me teeth out
I didn't have none in
Lost me Norman Wisdom's
Plus a trademark toothy grin
Pulled some out with pliers
What was left with sturdy string
A homeless voice
With not much choice
When scrounging from a bin
Now my gums have dentures
Three bridges and a stain
No more nights on pavements
But a heart that bares the pain

Homeless time at Christmas
Cold and far from hot
The lowest of society
That Santa Claus forgot
Lonely and unwanted
Confused and all alone
No bright festive grotto
That they can call their home
As revellers party
And affluent sing
To welcome the birth Of
a Bethlehem King
Tramps and hobos
Scavenge for salvation
Insulted and Abused
During times of jubilation
Wherever we come from
Whatever we see
Unopened presents
Under Somebody's tree
As the big day approaches
For one and for all
Sally Army lunch
In a disused hall
A thrown-together gift bag
A whistle and some tongue
Then back into the doorway
Where no carols will be sung
From a life of Destitution
Uncertainty and fear
A very Merry Christmas
And a prosperous New Year

I know a lop-eared rabbit
His name is Charlie Bowes
With great big floppy ears
And a tiny button-nose
His paws are size eleven
Plus a massive fluffy tail
He likes a Battered sausage
And lives in Maida Vale

A mouse came into my kitchen
And sat upon my knee
I asked him who he was
And what he wanted for his tea
He said his name was Norman
And jelly would be nice
So I did a little extra
Just to feed the other mice
He took his small containers
And left without a fuss
Then went back to his friends
Aboard a number 19 bus

A little dog went shopping
To see what he could get
Advised to eat more healthy
By a man who knows a vet
No more bacon sandwiches
With loganberry tart
Replace with tuna salad
And a griddled celery heart
Little dog seemed puzzled
As he nibbled on his bone
"Can't see what the problem is
'I'm only 19 stone"

A family clock struck midnight
Somewhere north of Fife
But noises were deciphered
As the toy box came to life
Train served at every station
Barbie stole the show
Just as the panda played Monopoly
With an ornamental crow
Building bricks sabre sticks bagatelle with pick and mix
The dolls tried table football
As the midnight clock struck six
Grown-ups were approaching
Reared an ugly head
So every toy jumped in the box
And clambered into bed

There was a little bear
Who had a little chair
He didn't do that much all day
And never seemed to care
His mother made his porridge
His father trimmed his locks
His sister cleaned his bedroom
And bundled up his socks
He wasn't keen on exercise
Nor tidying the garden
Every time he failed to show his family begged his pardon
Just sat all day and rubbed his tum
Whilst sitting quietly on his bum
Never went to the Barnet fair
Oh that lazy little bear

Never been to Reykjavik
Or attacked by an assailant
Never had Distempa
Or a cost of living payment
Never owned a Trouser press
Never Milked a bull
Never had a breakdown
Whilst on holiday in Hull
Never drove a tractor
Never boiled a trout
Never thought that flatulence
Is better in than out
Never borrowed sandals
Or baked a chicken pie
Nothing more to say
Goodbye

A little girl called Suzie
Woke up one Christmas morn
To a stocking full of presents
And a reindeer all forlorn
Santa had forgotten him
Abandoned in the street
A red nose rolling in the snow
And he couldn't find his feet
Suzie fetched him blankets
And a flask of herbal tea
You'd better come inside our house
Spend Christmas day with me
She sat him by the fire
Was frail and very old
Gave him roasted chestnuts
And some lockets for his cold
Rudolph stayed for festive lunch
Boy could this old fella munch
17 parsnips 19 spuds
Plus 27 Christmas puds
A moral note to Santa
When heading to Bavaria
Please count all your reindeer
Before you leave the area
Now safely reunited
With his master and his brood
The sleigh, it did not move one inch
'Coz he'd eaten too much food

A tiny little kitten
Couldn't have his cream
His mum she scrolled the Internet
Plus everywhere in Cheam
Nothing in the corner shop
Nothing going cheap
So he got back in his little bed
And cried himself to sleep

Harry the dalmatian
Was born without his spots
His back was bleak and empty
Not even tiny dots
His brothers and his sisters
Detecting an imposter
Advertised on eBay
And farmed him out for foster
Harry wasn't happy
Ecstatic not at all
He was a proper puppy
Who chased a tennis ball
So off he went to Brewers
To spend his pocket money
And painted spots upon his back
His belly and his tummy
From neither one nor the other
Now a loving little brother

Staying in a squat
Is like a trip to the Abyss
Contagious empty needles
And a bucket full of piss
Unpleasant undesirables
Grievous bodily harm
Rolling up a shirt sleeve
Whilst tightening their arm
Advantages are minimal
Nationalities eclectic
Everyone a criminal
No gas and no electric
This penitentiary sleepover
Is hardly heaven sent
Rat infested everywhere
But I didn't pay no rent
Eventually escaping
To expected jubilation
Underwent a treatment plan
And essential fumigation

When a circus came to Scarborough
Not one person wore a frown
Never seen an acrobat
Who gives you half a crown

Commencing at six thirty
We arrived at half past four
A ten-foot man on stilts turned up
To let us in the door

Three performing llamas
And a dancing chimpanzee
A man juggling bananas
Who came and sat with me

This season's act to top the polls
A tightrope walking cow
A back flip with two forward rolls
Three curtsey's and a bow

To make this marvellous thing complete
A jolly man with massive feet
With a big red nose, he's painted brown
Our effervescent circus clown

And so we left content and happy
Aunt Bertha almost wet her nappy
Decent folk without a care
As the circus came to Scarborough fair

Stood at bus stops in the rain
Debating If I'll ever see
Another one again
Next is shortly due
At just a quarter too
But will it be the 48
Or a number fifty two
The queue is getting bigger
This really is no fun day
According to the timetable
Last seen one month last Sunday
A transportation jobsworth
Surveys the sorry scene
Then appeared a handyman
Who keeps them nice and clean
With everybody angry
And close to spitting foam
We bought a box of cereal
And caught the milk float home

A rather burly spider
Walked straight into my house
Bigger than a goldfish
Slightly smaller than a mouse
He scuttled on the carpet
And settled on the wall
He was the biggest spider
I'd ever seen at all
My wife was in the garden
My cat was on the loo
Had he come to us on foot
Or escaped from London Zoo
Eventually, I caught him
And placed him in a jar
Spun a Web in our neighbour's shed
Then drove off in his car

My home town
A quirky place with Granny's high-on whizz
Mother's not a scooby who their daughter's father is
Vehicles with no wheels on
Bars on every door
High end fashion items
Hammered to the floor
Thieving at a premium
Profits at a loss
Dismissed by every corporation
Sacked by every boss
Fighting in the cul de sacs
Pissing in the street
Handy with their Fists
Useful with their feet
Vacancies for cash in hand
Waifs and strays and shirks
My manor and I love it
At least the Town Hall clock still works

Whilst I was a fat man
For breakfast had some chips
Could never comprehend the phrase
A lifetime on the hips
Couldn't find my tootsies
Rolled meself to bed
Nineteen Battered sausages
With seven loaves of bread
Condescending population
Challenged me at four
To line up my aim
And fit my frame
Through the nearest shithouse door
Advantage of obesity
If drinking pints of beer
Wouldn't lose me in a storm
And at least I know I'm here

Homeless and hungry
A sure-fire sign
Of a destitute person
In steady decline
Strolling streets for handouts
People stop and stare
At this prehistoric creature
With things inside his hair
He tries to make things better
Folks don't want to know
As the rain gets rather better
And the forecast mentions snow
His life is fraught with danger
Ambitions, they are damp
Away in any manger
Is no crib for any tramp
As he beds down for the evening
In a toilet or a skip
With the local villains scheming
He doesn't get much kip
And so this Vicious circle
With victims realistic
Churns out a fine example Of
a lengthening statistic

My twice-removed relation
Has a tendency to swear
In everything we do
He turns the atmosphere blue
Chucked out of establishment's
From Haywards Heath to Bude
A booming voice his language choice And
extremely bloody rude

Perhaps he has a problem
Can't keep it bottled In
A constant reel of blasphemy And
a liver soaked in gin
The art of confrontation
He has down to a tee
From shouting at a busker
To pissing in the sea

To kerb his foul mouth outbursts
And keep his job in shares
He gives two pounds to charity
Every time he Swears
Now the perfect gentleman
A fine upstanding bloke
Coz every time expletives flew
He'd end up stoney broke

A neanderthal from Scarborough
Was born in sixty-three
And quite coincidentally
That just happened to be me
In sixty four I broke the law
By fiddling stuff in Appledore
Which rocked the locals to the core
Precisely why they locked the door
Development was rapid
Adolescence bore some tricks
Impressed my uncle Benny
When I juggled sixteen bricks
Looking cute in dungarees
My father sailed the seven seas
From North Kentucky to Belize
Whilst I stayed home
And shot the breeze
At seven I predicted
An amazing opportunity
To challenge Edward Heath
And gain political immunity
A random act of kindness
That betrayed a whole community
Through the teenage years of adulthood
Convicted of affray
Which helped a bit
For the gormless twit I aspire to be today

If you dirtied Mother's bathroom
You sure did feel the wrath
With pot pourri in her laundry bin
And candles round the bath

Her tiles were shocking fushia
With beige and peanut grouting
When I pooed inside the bidet
She always starred shouting

Interiors matched the ceiling
Her toothbrush matched the floor
Finished off immaculately
By a mural on the door

Cleaning products all designer
Toilet brush from bristle
Cistern carved from the finest China
And a picture of a whistle

Should anybody chance a shave?
They dug themselves an early grave
A plughole all emaciated
A razor swiftly confiscated

So there we have me mam's latrine
Where brasses shine and surface gleam
She really did a smashing job
With no place for the urban yob

Get to work
Have no play
Such is life
A busy day
Eat an apple
Foil a raid
Buy some
Homemade lemonade
Stroke a puppy
Hatch a crime
Life is such a
Busy time
Eat Bananas
Drive a bus
Judith Chalmers
Bone a huss
Bend some treacle
Land a ship
Go to sleep
Inside a skip
All in all
A hectic day
But are we really
Made that way

My Dad went to hospital
Never came back
Broke a front bone
In the small of his back
My mother was shocked
The cat didn't care
Twenty-three pounds for
A tint in her hair
My sister was busy
The coroner seething
Cause of death
Wasn't breathing
Myself I'd gone fishing
In a watertight cave
So we buried him quickly
And danced on his grave

A tiny little donkey
With tears in his eyes
Couldn't quite believe
That someone stole his cherry
pies
He checked inside his stable
And underneath the hay
How could any person be so selfish In
that way
His mum was feeling bad for him
She went and bought some more
So donkey put a padlock on And
hid behind the door
Moral of this sordid tale
No sympathy no sorrow
Especially for piglet
Who is up in court tomorrow
These days our little donkey
Diminutive in size
Does after dinner speaking on
the pilfering of pies

For people created in Yorkshire
Be frugal and stick to the code
Don't pay for nowt you don't have to
Nor drop a meat pie on the road

When hailing a taxi to Filey
Remember it's cheaper to walk
Always refrain from catching the train
When planning a jolly in York

Take packet sugar from snack bars
Attach next door's tap to your hose
First to buy a round of drinks
When the bar's about to close

Never tip a waiter
Nor pay a penny more
Ensuring that your gotten gains
Are nailed beneath the floor

Are we paternally greedy?
A secret required to keep
Though I do stick my head right under the bed
To ascertain if I've lost any sleep

When I was a little boy
My shaver was a Ronson
Didn't care for Solitaire
Nor heard of Charlie Bronson
Every time I saw a sign
The ship went to the moon
Investigating nutmeg
And a helium balloon
Things got back to normal
Through a complimentary shipment
Of penguins dancing in the snow
And musical equipment
Really, not a clue
To whom this nonsense is aspiring
Don't hesitate to e-mail
As the shop is currently hiring.

Whilst in an open prison
Came and went just as I please
Visited the town in case the guvnor needed cheese
Often had a sauna
If I should be so bold
Complained in joined-up writing
If the temperature was cold
Up to date gymnasium
Chandeliers of glass
Not one inmate fiddled with me
Up the Khyber Pass
Assigned a valet butler
To titillate my shrub
Vanilla in the custard
Proper parsnips in the grub
To sum up my experience
Enjoyed the place to bits
Bigger than the Ivy
Slightly better than the Ritz

Ejected from establishments
From John 'O Groats to Putney
From putting toilet windows through
To poisoning the chutney
Pool cue violation
Intimidation fear
Failure to communicate
And pissing in the beer
One too many sherbets
A belly full of Baileys
Belting people on the head
With several ukuleles
Making hats with drip trays
Impersonating rain
To be met with those immortal words
And don't come back again

A rabbit woke one Christmas
To find he couldn't see
No Advent Calendar images
No presents near the tree
His siblings were excited
New bikes around the park
But Cecil simply sat there
A bunny in the dark
Why was he in darkness
Why his eyesight dim
Only to discover
He forgot to put them in
So restoration Christmas
And no more weeping willow
Leave them in the sockets
Not beside you on the pillow

To prepare the perfect pudding
You have to cut the mustard
Don't curdle the ingredients
Or beat the eggs to custard
Set the oven early
To get the timing right
Then add a Curly Wurly
Which gives an extra bite
When rolling out your pastry
Don't hesitate to stop
Sift self-rising flour
Then purchase from a shop
So there you have your method
A recipe within
So when it turns out golden black
Just chuck it in the bin

As I gaze a Sussex coastline
I don't belong, it isn't mine
Wish I was in Yorkshire by the sea
They don't encourage Bingo
Criticise my lingo
Yearn to be in Yorkshire by the sea
Don't serve chips with gravy
Nor Dance to "In The Navy"
Want to be in Yorkshire by the sea
I'm just a gormless Northern twit
Don't leave the bath to have a shit
Long to be in Yorkshire by the sea
No mushy peas no builder's tea
Could be in Leeds for half past three
Oh to be in Yorkshire by the sea

I'm no vindictive person
Despite the wicked rumours
Despite several muck ups
Cock ups and bloomers
Give a bit to charity
Always petting dogs
Ambassador for clarity
Protecting orphaned frogs
Hand a child a shilling
Pick litter off the floor
Priority for females
When I'm opening a door
Never been an angel
Nor classed as a Biblical Saint
Served my time
Committed a crime
When Pilfering upside down paint
Assist an old lady
Bake her a pie
Pull out a plum
What a good egg am I

Change at Bedlam
Change at Crewe
Where the carriages
Are painted blue
Don't understand
The on board pronouncements
Listen to station staff for announcements
Leaves on the line
Technical malfunction
Suicidal tendencies
A network up the junction
Ticket inspector
Hasn't got a clue
That Bradford City won three two
Where a replacement bus service
Will carry on to Looe
With an out of order toilet
And nothing much to do
Eventually stranded in
A rural railway station
Many miles away
From your chosen destination
With everyone on strike
It's quicker by bike
As your Plymouth train is running late
In a suburb twinned with New Cross Gate

My 1980s' ego
Was 27 stone
19 double vodkas
Then I steamrolled home alone
Toppled in the garden
Fell over the cat
Then mother smacked me
Round the head
With next door's cricket bat
A decade deft of no control
No trade no prospects
On the whole
Of getting shifted off the dole
My apprenticeship for homelessness
Was served in clubs and bars
For scavenging in dustbins
And sleeping under stars

No Christmas tree
No baubles blue
No presents in a row
No statutory holly Bush
Nor frolics in the snow
No messages from Rudolph
Just a bedroom on a seat
A spiral of if onlys
And a jar of potted meat
Unaware what day it is
No jingle all the way No
Christmas for the homeless
As they put their dreams away.

Busting for a wee wee
Can prove so inconvenient
Emptying a bladder
That is full and disobedient
Late for an appointment
Or picking up a ship
All because your urine
Overflows a builder's skip
Whether Southend on sea
To be dying for a pee
A specialist must be called
Or a catheter installed
Law courts cinque ports
Fill your boots and stain your shorts
Please go before departing
A humble small abode
No indecisive farting
On a fairly clean commode
So before you visit once or twice
Heed a little sound advice
If you sprinkle when you tinkle
Please be sweet and wipe the seat

To be a famous astronaut
Is something I could do
Analysed by Patrick Moore
In a TV interview

Return home with memento's
And sell them in a shop
Fifty pence a crater
Many more for lumps of rock

Become a huge celebrity
The whole world in my pocket
Just because I've seen the moon
From the cockpit of a rocket

Talks on atmospheric stuff
To higher education
Whilst surviving on potcheen and snuff
In a solar situation

Relive the expedition
On some channel four promotion
From claustrophobic capsule
To my splashdown in the ocean

Sadly never happen
To a nobody like me
As I peer through life's telescope
Whilst on holiday in Torquay

An abiding childhood memory
Excitement through and through
My holidays to Cayton Bay
And the bus was painted blue

Blimey yikes the three wheeled bikes
A caravan for my bed
Kids wore painted faces
And a doodah on their head

Days were hectic days were peach
Burying father on the beach
Building castles sifting sand
Awaiting Gristhorpe's marching band

Ice cream was extremely yummy
As it nestled in our bulging tummy
Crazy golf and cardboard ships
On Friday we had fish and chips

One night it really thundered
Rattled all our doorway
Knocking Bertha off her bricks
We were on our way Norway

Last night always party time
A right extravaganza
Prizes games and petty crime
Dancing to Mario Lanza

Morning campers time to depart
By train or plane or horse and cart
Leave all luggage by a gate
For the big blue bus, which is never late

What permits the snotty gits
To stand and have a pop
Just because I purchase clothes
From a local charity shop
Just because they way up high
And I am down below
With gazing eyes
They criticise
My second hand feather bedspread
With matching duck down throw
I steam the undergarments
On a boil wash and a swill
Three sessions with the washboard
And a hand me down power drill
The affluent they giggle
As I wander down the way
In safari suit and pixie boot
And a shirt from C&A
A chandelier with attitude
A porcelain piglet in the nude
An item classed as very crude
A 17th century map of Bude
All in a day searching handouts and pine
Which posh boy can shove
Where the sun doesn't shine

The day I checked in to The Ritz
I ordered trout and cheesy chips
Didn't have the lemon tea
As its doesn't quite agree with me
All the guests had loads of money
Apart from little me
Spoke to a self made magnate
Whilst on a posh settee
Decor was fantastic
With good stuff on the wall
A painting from Picasso
And a bust by Bobby Ball
One professionally oiled hospitality machine
With free range eggs and squirty cream
Best ever looking after team
From Tunbridge Wells to Aberdeen
And so my stay had ended
No souvenir flower
No time to be befriended
As my budget only stretched to bit and an hour

When I came out as nutty
Mother couldn't comprehend
How could any son of hers
Be halfway round the bend
I knew she would support me
Right until the bitter end
Especially as a pine nut
Was my best forever friend
With blood tests inconclusive
And gravy on the knee
Officially announced that
Adolf Hitler was a tree
Psychologist was clueless
Further tests returned unclear
Which left me slightly scrumpy
With a banana in me ear
The local congregation
Offered cob nuts and some chains
Just as me mam suggested
That I be wired to the mains
There must be a solution
The female blacksmith cried
So just to make things interesting
She placed a gerbil on the side
With an institution calling
The facility correction
A doctor put my mind at rest
With a rhubarb juice infection
Moral of my trumpet
Never fry your middle wrist
'Coz if you trouble double ten
Could end up round the twist

Suicide is painless
Succeeded at it twice
Once mission is accomplished
It really is quite nice
Relaxing in a coffin
In a dignified dead heap
Awaiting friends and family
To say you only look asleep
A man in black looks after you
Potentially a druid
Rubs your tum
And fills your bum
With rich embalming fluid
Once they turn the lights out
The stiffs begin to tire
As they dream of going in the hole
Or head first in a fire

A tiny bear came to up me
Whilst fishing on The Rhine
Offered me a jelly bean
Enquired about the time
I told him it was five past two
As he'd missed his train
To outside Crewe
Lost his money on the bus
Spent the rest in Toys R Us
He asked me nicely for a cuddle
As he'd got himself in
A spot of trouble
I asked him who he was
Whilst attempting to assist
His name was Cyril Bumpkin
And he'd never once been kissed
After eating all his ice cream cone
I found a way to get him home
Starting at Bristol
Kingston and Cheam
We thumbed a lift to Aberdeen
Turning left at Wigan
We went to Tunbridge Wells
Where Bunty Bear was waiting
To the sound of wedding bells
He thank me prior
To going on his way
To a luxury honeymoon
In Montego Bay

Sprouts are cylindrical
Sprouts can be fun
Sprouts affect the decibels
Omitted from your bum
Kids don't really like them
Babies make them scream
These crunchy tasteless bullets
Which are painted Lincoln green
But if mother refuses to buy them
As a vegetable Yuletide addition
Mutiny hits coz we love them to bits
They are part of the Christmas tradition

Christmas time
The kids want gifts
Dad's overtime and extra shifts
Mother eyes a bogof deal
To place them on an even keel
Shops are full of tempting toys
For lots of eager girls and boys
The latest doll
A must have thing
Something that can dance and sing
Arthur will get nothing
Coz the girl next door he kissed
Rudolph was informed
Therefore he crossed him off the list
Food costs a fortune
At competitive rates
Why, oh why
Do we always purchase dates
December 25th arrives
And so it came to pass
If lazy bones from Greenland Ever
moves his big fat arse

Sorry I'm not working
An engineer is on his way
Developed man flu symptoms
Won't be doing much today
Informed the boss
Who isn't keen
Because my tongue is turning green
With spots on my face
And lumps on my snout
I may need to have my adenoids out
My prostrate inflamed
From a dislocated cavity
Colleagues celebrating my
Impressive punctuality
I Leap out of bed
Feeling 16 foot tall
Before sensing there is really
Nothing wrong with me at all.

My parents owned a naughty dog
He ate a candelabra
Destroyed the alabaster pots
And lived with us in Scarborough
His name was Tiger Lily
You chew that if you dare
His cousin's name was Billy
And he lived across the square
Destroyed the garden furniture
To get his point across
A proper little whirlwind
Mam's Pug Alsatian Cross
Barred from dog behaviour class
Wiped his arse with broken glass
Launched a cooker to the sky
Cutting off our gas supply
Got fruity with a poodle
In the ornamental bidet
Now void of doggy day care
And up for sale one bay

I bought a Christmas jumper
With Ruldoph on my back
Santa on the front
Complete with bushy beard and sack
Wore it for a party
As festive people do
A colour coded evening
Fronting bogey green and blue
Elves were in attendance
Two reindeer's in a stable
Little donkey drank the lot
And fell straight through a table
Took all my clothes off
To "Simply the Best"
Revealing rancid boxer shorts
And a Marks & Spencer vest
Jackdaws trap doors Bugs Bunny and Thumper
Oh that naughty Christmas jumper

If every dog was human
What a wonderful world it would be
No stereotypical mood swings
No bodies adrift in the sea
Loyalty would be contagious
With an unconditional sway
Cuddle abundance outrageous
As they stand by your side every day
Never question never judgemental
Fiercely loyal till the end
If every dog was human
We would have a forever best friend

I possess an old friend
Kneecaps Norman
From the school of
Soft bruises and knocks
Reached fifty nine
So I sent him
Some wine
Which he couldn't remove
From the box
They didn't provide
No instructions
Or a manual
Which helped him
To think
Not good for a man
With no master plan
Who desperately needed
A drink
I told him to fetch
A large hammer
Plus a massive cylindrical saw
So he tickled his tum
Walloped a thumb
And ended up flat on the floor
Eventually managed to shift it
With the aid of an elephant's trunk
Laid back with some snacks
But wouldn't relax
Till the whole fucking
Lot had been sunk

As evening clouds they lengthen And heavy raindrops fall
Just what Tomorrow has in store
We've no idea at all
We can't predict the future
Circumnavigate the streams
A lifetime catches up with us
Destroying all our hopes
Criticising all our dreams
With twilight times upon us
Regret is a pointless commodity
As I come to an end
Not a family or friend
My remains in the hands
Of a local authority
As the padre and parishioner
Were crying for my soul
Announced it was the first time
That I'd been off the dole
So they stuck me in the pulpit
And dug a bigger hole

Printed by BoD™in Norderstedt, Germany